The Fabulous and Fun World of Chemistry
A science book for girls by girls!!

Angela Taha Naef, PhD
Adria Taha-Resnick, M.A. Ed.
Designed by Jeno Design

RAINBOW COLORS ON YOUR FINGERS & TOES!

We can paint the world with our imagination and paint our nails with chemistry!

Nail polish is a fun way to add color and protection to your nails. Polish works based on the chemicals in the mixture. The key ingredient is a <u>polymer</u> called nitrocellulose cotton which is a liquid with small cotton fibers. In nail polish the nitrocellulose cotton is dissolved in a liquid called a <u>solvent</u> that keeps the nitrocellulose <u>polymer</u> as a liquid until you are ready to paint your nails so that it can go on smooth and cover your entire nail. During the time when your nails are drying the liquid <u>solvent</u> <u>evaporates</u> and the nitrocellulose is left behind creating a solid that sticks to your nails. Be careful during the drying time so you don't smudge your fresh manicure or pedicure.

Nail polish has other chemicals in it, too; things to make the polish stick better, things to make it dry faster, and, of course, color.

Today we can paint our nails lots of different colors. We can paint them clear too to make them nice and shiny! We can add stripes, dots, and even paint a heart or rainbow!

Hi! I'm Daisy and I'm so excited to share the wonderful world of Chemistry with you!

3

DID YOU KNOW?

The art of nail coloring has been around for centuries and goes back to ancient lands in China, Egypt, and India. The science of nail polish is a <u>chemist</u>'s dream! Nail polish goes from a liquid in the bottle to a solid right in front of our eyes.

BATH TIME!

BEAUTIFUL

& CLEAN

HAIR!

Bubbles, suds, and lather – how do they make your hair so soft, clean, and smell so nice?

Washing our hair with shampoo is something we do all the time and there are lots of options in the stores! Some smell different with fragrances added. Some look different with different colors added. So what do they all have in common? The answer is in the chemistry of the shampoo and how it interacts with the chemistry of your hair.

The key ingredient in shampoo is called a detergent. A detergent is a type of surfactant. A surfactant is a molecule that can mix with both water and oil. When you put shampoo on your wet hair, the surfactant attaches on to the oil that has built up on your scalp and hair. It is this oil, called sebum, that makes your hair dirty! Sebum is naturally produced by your scalp to protect your hair, but it also collects dirt from the playground and dry skin flakes that naturally come off our scalp. Over time, too much dirt accumulates and we need to wash our hair. Here is where shampoo comes in; it can attach to the dirt and sebum and then it can all be washed away when we add water to rinse out the shampoo.

Shampoo also has perfumes added that are left behind after rinsing leaving your hair smelling fresh and clean. Some shampoo makers add in different pigments, or colors, to give hair a shiny appearance.

After we shampoo, we also add conditioner to our hair to make it easier to comb and style. Conditioners are made of different chemicals that can moisturize and repair damaged hair. The moisturizing effect comes from a chemical called a humectant. Humectants love water and hold moisture to your hair so that it does not become dry and brittle. To make hair look glossy and shiny, conditioner has molecules that reflect light on your hair. It's like having a whole bunch of tiny little mirrors on each strand of hair!

DID YOU KNOW?

Before the invention of shampoo, people washed their hair with rice husk and rice straw. The husks and straw were burned into ash and mixed with water to form a lather which was then scrubbed into the hair.

ICE
CREAM
IS VERY COOL
CHEMISTRY!

All over the world, people enjoy ice cream in a cup, in a cone, with sprinkles, chocolate syrup, or whatever their hearts desire! To make homemade ice cream all you need are a few simple ingredients : milk, sugar, flavorings or fruit, ice, and salt. The magic behind ice cream is the salt! The salt is added to the ice and placed around the bowl or bag that you will use to make the ice cream.

The reason salt is so important is that you need to cool the ingredients to a cold enough temperature to make the mixture turn from liquid to a solid. Just using ice alone will not get the mixture cold enough, so we add salt to the ice to lower its freezing point temperature. The most typical salt used is sodium chloride, NaCl, and it works because when it dissolves in the ice water it breaks into 2 ionic particles (Na^+ and Cl^-) and makes it really tough for water molecules to form ice. You can buy 'ice cream salt', which are just large crystals instead of the small crystals you see in your salt shaker at home. It takes longer for the bigger salt crystals to dissolve and that gives you more time to evenly stir or shake and cool the mixture into a yummy ice cream treat!

Liquid nitrogen can be used to freeze ice cream too – very fast and VERY cold! Liquid nitrogen (N_2) is over 200 degrees colder than the salt-ice mixture and when you mix it with the ice cream ingredients it freezes on contact!

TRY IT WITH DAISY!

Make ice cream

What you'll need:
- 1 tablespoon sugar
- 1/2 cup milk or half & half
- 1/4 teaspoon vanilla
- 6 tablespoons rock salt
- 1 pint-size plastic food storage bag
- 1 gallon-size plastic food storage bag
- Ice cubes

How to make it:
1. Fill the large bag half full of ice and add the rock salt. Seal the bag.
2. Put milk, vanilla, and sugar into the small bag and seal it.
3. Place the small bag inside the large one and seal it again carefully.
4. Shake until the mixture is ice cream which takes about 5 minutes.
5. Wipe off the top of the small bag and open it carefully. Enjoy!

DID YOU KNOW?

True ice cream recipes first appeared in 18th century England and America.

YOUR SANDWICH HAS GAS! WELL THAT'S KIND OF GROSS....

Ever wonder why bread rises when it is made?
It's all in the chemistry of yeast!

Yeast is a live, single-celled fungus that is added to bread to make it airy and light. In chemical terms, bread is a kind of foam – lots of connecting parts with holes in it like a sponge. The holes are made by special kinds of sugars that undergo a chemical reaction and release <u>carbon dioxide</u> (CO_2) in the bread dough. Carbon dioxide is a gas and bubbles through the dough leaving behind different sized holes.

Another way to make the gas is to combine chemicals that, when in contact with water and heat, undergo a chemical reaction. This is called chemical leavening. Some chemical leaveners are baking soda, baking powder, and cream of tartar.

Some of your favorite foods, like muffins, pancakes, and biscuits are made using chemical leaveners.

TRY IT WITH DAISY!

Inflate a balloon with yeast gas!

What you'll need:
- 1 packet of active dry yeast
- 1 cup very warm water (105° F–115° F)
- 2 tablespoons sugar
- 1 large rubber balloon
- 1 small (1-pint to 1-liter) empty water bottle

How to make it:

1. Stretch out the balloon by blowing it up several times and set aside.

2. Mix the packet of yeast and the sugar in the cup of warm water and stir.

3. After the yeast and sugar have dissolved, pour the mix into the water bottle. You'll see chemistry in action with bubbles forming as the yeast produces carbon dioxide.

4. Next attach the balloon to the top of the water bottle.

5. After just a few minutes the balloon will start to inflate!

DID YOU KNOW?

There are over 500 species of yeast and they are all alive! They are part of the fungi kingdom. Make sure you do not eat raw, active yeast because it will react in your stomach and create a lot of gas.

SUGAR!
IT MAKES LIFE
SO SWEET!

There are many different types of sugar and they come from many different sources. Sugars are simple carbohydrates that the body uses to create energy in a process called metabolism. Your body stores sugar molecules as energy so you can run, play, and do your homework!

There are different types of sugar molecules that are made up of similar atoms but have different numbers of those atoms.The building blocks are called saccharides and there are monosaccharides ("mono" means one), disaccahrides ("di" means two), trisaccharides ("tri" means three) and even larger ones. Two important monosaccharies are glucose and fructose. Glucose is the sugar that your body uses for energy. Fructose is the sugar found in fruits and vegetables like melons, berries, potatoes, and onions. The most common sugar we have every day is sucrose and it is a disaccharide. This is the sugar you might use on your cereal and it comes from sugar cane and sugar beets.

The sweetness of sugars depends on the molecular structure. Fructose (fruit sugar) is about two times more sweet than sucrose (table sugar) and about ten times more sweet than lactose (milk sugar).

TRY IT WITH DAISY!

Here's a recipe for some sweet rock candy!

What you'll need:
- 4 cups sugar
- 1 cup water
- food coloring
- clean glass jar
- 3-5 - 6 inch string pieces
- pencil

How to make it:

1. In a medium saucepan, heat 2 cups of the sugar and the water. Do not boil! Stir until the sugar is completely dissolved – a wood spoon works best. Gradually add a few drops of the food coloring of your choice (purple is my favorite!) and the additional sugar, stirring continuously until all the sugar is dissolved.

2. Next pour it into a clean glass jar and tie the pieces of string to the pencil and suspend them across the mouth of the jar so that the ends hang into the sugar water.

3. Crystals will form in about an hour and pieces can be broken off and eaten – yum! Bigger crystals will grow if you leave it for a few days or even a week! It is really fun to watch them slowly grow and even more fun to have a sweet treat!

THE MAGICAL
PERIODIC
TABLE
OF THE ELEMENTS

Every <u>chemist</u> just falls in love with the periodic table of the elements – it is where the world of <u>chemistry</u> all comes together! The history of the periodic table dates back to the 1860's when Dmitri Mendeleev constructed it to explain the order of elements from lightest to heaviest. At the time he created the chart, only about half of the elements were included because many of them had not been discovered yet! Even today scientists are discovering new elements.

DID YOU KNOW? ↖

An element on the periodic table is described by letter symbol and numbers that explain the characteristics of the element. The number at the top of the box is the atomic number and represents the number of protons in the atom nucleus and the number at the bottom of the box represents the relative atomic mass of the atom. The first element of the periodic table is hydrogen and has the symbol H. It is the lightest of all elements with a relative atomic mass of only 1.008.

1

H

1.008

PERIODIC TABLE OF THE ELEMENTS

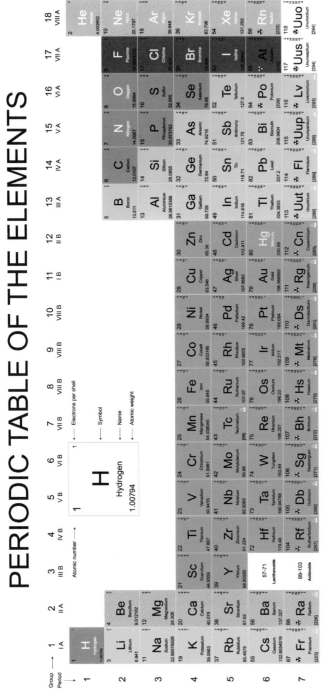

Glossary

Alkaline- adj. Of, relating to, or containing an alkali. Having a pH greater than 7. Having a low concentration of hydrogen ions.

Atoms- n. A part or particle considered to be an irreducible constituent of a specified system. An extremely small part, quantity, or amount.

Carbohydrates- n. Any of a group of organic compounds that includes sugars, starches, celluloses, and gums and serves as a major energy source in the diet of animals. These compounds are produced by photosynthetic plants and contain only carbon, hydrogen, and oxygen.

Carbon dioxide- n. A colorless, odorless, incombustible gas, CO_2, formed during respiration, combustion, and organic decomposition and used in food refrigeration, carbonated beverages, inert atmospheres, fire extinguishers, and aerosols. Also called carbonic acid gas.

Chemist- n. A scientist specializing in chemistry.

Chemistry- n. The science of the composition, structure, properties, and reactions of matter, especially of atomic and molecular systems. The composition, structure, properties, and reactions of a substance.

Compound- n. A pure, macroscopically homogeneous substance consisting of atoms or ions of two or more different elements in definite proportions that cannot be separated by physical means.

Evaporate- v. To convert or change into a vapor.

Humectant- n. A substance that promotes retention of moisture.

Ionic- adj. Of, containing, or involving charged particles (ions).

Metabolism- n. The chemical processes occurring within a living cell or organism that are necessary for the maintenance of life. In metabolism some substances are broken down to yield energy for vital processes while other substances, necessary for life, are synthesized.

Molecule- n. The smallest particle of a substance that retains the chemical and physical properties of the substance and is composed of two or more atoms; a group of like or different atoms held together by chemical forces. A small particle; a tiny bit.

Nitrogen- n. A nonmetallic element that constitutes nearly four-fifths of the air by volume, occurring as a colorless, odorless, almost inert diatomic gas.

Polymer- n. Any of numerous natural and synthetic compounds of usually high molecular weight consisting of up to millions of repeated linked units, each a relatively light and simple molecule.

Saccharides- n. any of a large group of carbohydrates, including all sugars and starches. Almost all carbohydrates are saccharides.

Sebum- n. The semifluid secretion of the sebaceous glands, consisting chiefly of fat, keratin, and cellular material.

Sodium chloride- n. A colorless or white crystalline compound, NaCl, used in the manufacture of chemicals and as a food preservative and seasoning.

Solvent- adj. A substance in which another substance is dissolved, forming a solution. A substance, usually a liquid, capable of dissolving another substance.

Sucrose- n. A crystalline disaccharide of fructose and glucose, found in many plants but extracted as ordinary sugar mainly from sugar cane and sugar beets, widely used as a sweetener or preservative.

Surfactant- n. A substance that tends to reduce the surface tension of a liquid in which it is dissolved so the liquid spreads out instead of forming droplets.

ABOUT THE BOOK
The Smarty Skirts series is inspired by two sisters who believe that girls can be motivated to love science by seeing it in their everyday lives.

ABOUT THE AUTHORS
Adria Taha-Resnick is a college professor with over 23 years of experience working with young children. She has degrees in Childhood Development and Early Childhood Education and is a well-respected and active member in the Early Childhood Education community. She lives in Southern California with her husband and two daughters.

Angela Taha Naef has fostered her innate love for science into a rewarding career in science & technology which has spanned 20 years. She has a Ph. D. in Chemistry, is an inventor on several patents and has been recognized with awards for new product development. She lives in Denmark with her husband and two children.

Printed in Great Britain
by Amazon

29284869R00016